MARTIN H. BUSH is Assistant Dean for Academic Resources at Syracuse University where he has been instrumental in developing wide support for the University's scholarship, art and manuscript programs. He is also the author of BEN SHAHN: THE PASSION OF SACCO AND VANZETTI and REVOLUTIONARY ENIGMA, a story of General Philip Schuyler during the American Revolution.

MARYA ZATURENSKA was awarded the Pulitzer Prize in 1938 for her second book of poems entitled: COLD MORNING SKY. Besides seven books of verse she has written a biography of Christina Rossetti and has collaborated with her husband, the poet and critic Horace Gregory, in writing A HISTORY OF AMERICAN POETRY, 1900-1940.

DOMINIC BEVAN WYNDHAM LEWIS is a notable English biographer and the original "Beachcomber" of the DAILY EXPRESS who delighted readers with his column of runcible characters and whimsical comment. His fifteenth and latest book, THE WORLD OF GOYA, was published last year. He now lives near Alicante, Spain.

Distributed by
Syracuse University Press
Box 8, University Station
Syracuse, New York 13210

D1288510

doris caesar

doris caesar

by Martin H. Bush

with a Preface by D.B. Wyndham Lewis

and an Introduction by Marya Zaturenska
Pulitzer Prize for Poetry | 1938

Bibliography and Index by Lynn Candace DeSilvey | Syracuse University

"It is the strength in people that moves me. The wonderful power to handle and accept, or, if not to accept, to beat."

Doris Caesar

MÄDCHEN.
1966. Bronze. 54 high.

For Lisa, Jennifer and Pamela, my daughters

Measurements in the captions are in inches. Height precedes width
except in the case of sculpture, where the largest dimension is given.

FORM
Three dimensional
Solid
Massive
I love to feel the clay
In my nails,
I love the strong muscles
In my fingers
And the tired ache
That comes from work
Too hard,
I love the dirty overall
And cold
North light
And the feel of clay.

Form
Three dimensional
Solid
Massive
I hate my hands
That cannot do
My will,
I hate the years that pass
And hurry by
And leave me
With the feel of clay.
I hate my soul
That clings
Too close to me,
I want to put it
In a piece of clay.

Doris Caesar

STANDING WOMAN, hands down in back.
1962. Bronze. 44 high.

SEATED WOMAN, arms on knees.
1963. Bronze. 20 high.

ASCENT.
1957. Brass. 60 high.

STANDING WOMAN.
1962. Bronze. 38 high.

PREFACE

With considerable diffidence, I venture to prelude my friend Martin Bush's survey of Doris Caesar's work, for which I have the sincerest admiration, with some brief reflection on the evolution of the nude.

The golden age of the nude began with the Renaissance and ended with the eighteenth century, to which fact Titian's "Venus" and one of Francisco Goya's "Majas" testify. The hallmark of these two celebrated charmers is opulence of contour and a eupeptic content. Life is good to them and their contours have a kind of sheen on their ample flesh.

The nineteenth century saw the advent of the steam engine and a marked decline in the status of the nude. Outside the Latin countries, their prestige so declined that in Britain many connoisseurs preferred Sir Edwin Landseer's stags.

Today, as one perceives from Doris Caesar's world, they suffer all the despairs and malignancies of the age of the atomic bomb, and the effect on their physique is significant. Many of them are five to seven feet high, excessively emaciated, and their small faces bear all the stigmata of dislike and disgust. Elongation is in itself not unaesthetic. In the celebrated basilica at Vezelay, France, the effect of those slender piers of undecorated stone springing to the distant roof is entirely lovely.

STANDING WOMAN, hands outstretched.
1964. Bronze. 10 high.

The human form as elongated by Doris Caesar seems to lack magic. But of course they are not there to charm. A pair of dancers of excessively emaciated contours and enigmatic features appears to be crying for help rather than expressing the joys of spring. The seated figure with the smallest of heads and arms dwindling to practically nothing seems to be more than a monument to inexplicable despair. A long maternal figure with strange feet is contemplating a child of curiously normal shape. On the other hand, a female figure of almost no eccentricity is gracious and charming.

So much—or so little—for Mrs. Caesar's figures. The craftsmanship involved is quite superb, and the satire relentless. A traveller lately in Indonesia tells me that her art appears to have some affinity with a traditional sculpture of those parts. The Renaissance would not have conceivably understood it, though I think the Goya of the *Caprichos* would have appreciated it, having created a few gargoyles himself. One may also strive to guess what John Ruskin—whose proclamation inspired much earnest labour when he declared that the function of art is to recall the moral energies of a nation to forgotten duties—would have said about Doris Caesar in a new encyclical. For myself, I would only presume to say that as an artist and a satirist she is unique, agreeably acid and wholly arresting.

March, 1969

D.B. Wyndham Lewis
Alicante, Spain

LOTUS FLOWER.
1960. Bronze. 50 high.

FORM.
1963. Bronze. 18 high.

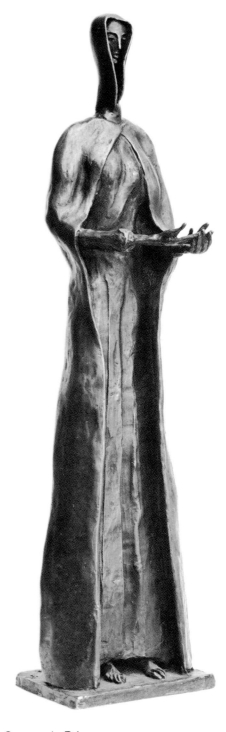

ST. THERESE OF LISIEUX.
1962. Bronze. 27 high. Collection of St. Gregory's Priory,
Three Rivers, Michigan.

INTRODUCTION

I have long been interested in the problem—I suppose it is a problem—of the limited achievement of women in the arts. So many are called, so few are chosen. In literature, where they have done the most, they have at least produced a Jane Austen, an Emily Brontë, a Colette in France, an Anna Akhmatova in Russia. Whatever one may say of their ultimate greatness, they are invaluable, they are truly unique. I speak only of those whose work at its best breathes a sensitive, an illuminating, an authentic femininity. There are none comparable to these names in musical composition or even in painting and art—in which women have always been encouraged, if only as a charming social accomplishment, like playing the piano. Even Queen Victoria did a number of competent sketches, not touched up we hope, by too loyal instructors.

Doris Caesar is feminine in the best sense. She is by natural fine taste and instinct most truly herself. She surmounts the difficulties of her art and her sex, and the art she has chosen has all the "fascination of the difficult." In doing this she has given to her sculptures a sensitive, an almost lyric delicacy of movement. Of course she has her influences, she is not underivative—who is? But her masters are among the best, for here again her fine taste and instincts have guided her. I see Lehmbrück, Giacometti, and even Henry Moore, but in her best work their experiences are her own, they are thoroughly assimilated. She is neither facile, pretty, nor too fashionable—all flaws of the woman artist. There is penetration and self knowledge in her figures, especially when she attempts the female form. Then she often catches a quality rare enough in all the arts today— a sense of beauty! I do not think these sculptures will date when at their most successful; they have a timeless quality, of that art which speaks for every epoch and always seems fresh.

I cannot say that I always like all of her work. She sometimes fails because she is over-ambitious and attempts too much. But when she lets her sensibility and trained instincts guide her, something is achieved that is art. Nothing can be more beautiful than her "Seated Woman" done in 1960, which has solidity as well as style. Even more interesting is her "Seated Torso," where all is harmony and inner strength. It is a truly moving work of art, for the figure seems both fragile and strong. It has poetic insight.

Doris Caesar's art reminds me, though curiously, of another woman—a painter who died in Germany in 1907, at an early age, but who is being slowly rediscovered today. This was Paula Modersohn-Becker, on whose death the poet Rilke wrote one of his most beautiful elegies.

Doris Caesar's art is unlike hers in many ways. I do not imply a comparison in kind. Paula Modersohn-Becker before her death had tried to achieve a certain ruggedness and force— natural enough when one remembers that she had just discovered Cézanne long before he became fashionable. But she and Doris Caesar have this in common: an unmistakable feminine sensibility and strength, a touch of pathos, an inner intensity. The resemblance, of course, is purely spiritual, one of tempermental affinity. But this affinity also accounts for their strange individuality.

One feels that Doris Caesar, like Paula Modersohn-Becker, will always be rediscovered.

March, 1969   Marya Zaturenska
                                               Palisades, New York

SEATED WOMAN.
1960. Bronze. 32 high. Collection of the Syracuse University
Museum of Art, Syracuse, New York.

KNEELING WOMAN, sitting on heels.
1962. Bronze. 5¼ high.

FOREWORD
AND
ACKNOWLEDGEMENTS

When I first met Doris Caesar in the autumn of 1963, it occurred to me that she would make a fine subject for a book since her work was not sufficiently known to the general public. But six years were to pass before I followed that first impulse. During that time Syracuse University acquired the largest single collection of her sculpture for its art museum. The University also established a Doris Caesar Manuscript Collection in its manuscript division, which has the largest and finest collection of artists' papers in the United States. I had the privilege of arranging these acquisitions for Syracuse, and now I have had the pleasure of preparing a book about this truly remarkable woman.

In the course of writing this volume, I have acquired many obligations. Most of all, I am deeply grateful to Doris Caesar for making available her manuscripts, notes, letters, clippings and biographical materials, and to Harry Caesar, for providing me with useful insights about her work.

I especially want to thank Vice Chancellor Frank P. Piskor of Syracuse University for his continued active interest in my work.

There are many others I wish to thank: Marya Zaturenska for her fine introduction and D. B. Wyndham Lewis for his preface; Austin G. Paulnack for his astute comments on the manuscript; John I.H. Baur, Director of the Whitney Museum of American Art, for permission to quote extensively from his essay on the artist, which appeared in a book entitled *Four American Expressionists;* Martin Fass and Richard Wilson for their thoughtful suggestions; and my secretaries, Martha Holt and Lynn C. DeSilvey, who saw the manuscript through every stage with interest and good humor.

I would also like to express my appreciation to those individuals who assisted me in various ways, particularly Mr. and Mrs. Lester Francis Avnet, Mrs. Karen Bakke, Linda Buettner, Mrs. Seth Dennis, Jack Ericson, Robert Kerns, Mrs. Sam Langsdorf, Arnold Newman, John Nolan, Dr. Laurence Schmeckebier, Glen Skillin, Richard K. Tanzmann, Richard Underwood and Mrs. Ruth Zierler.

Finally I would like to thank the many private collectors and museums who made available information about Doris Caesar's sculptures and permitted me to reproduce them here. Unfortunately they are too numerous to be listed in this foreword, but their names appear elsewhere in the book.

April, 1969   Martin H. Bush

PROUD SEED.
1957. Bronze. 55 high.

WOMAN, on one knee.
1958. Bronze. 15 high.

DORIS CAESAR

Life is unhurried in Litchfield, Connecticut. There are no supermarkets, no neon signs, and no office workers rushing to a subway or hailing a speeding cab. It is quiet. On an autumn day the rustle of leaves overhead is more noticeable than the traffic that moves almost silently through town.

Litchfield is typically New England. Giant elm trees and graceful white houses line streets where Ethan Allen, Aaron Burr and other Revolutionary War heroes once lived. It was here also that Oliver Wolcott established America's first law school and trained some of our most distinguished leaders. Although Wolcott's school no longer exists, the village has not changed much over the years. Visitors still feel a sense of history when passing "whipping post" elm or the Congregationalist Church near the village green.

Newcomers might assume that there is little that is really modern in Litchfield. But this would be far from the truth. A chance meeting with a lovely resident, still youthful in her mid-seventies, would soon change their minds. Each morning she emerges from a magnificent white house built in 1792, crosses the village green, perhaps stopping to chat for a moment with a neighbor, then enters Cobble Court and disappears into a quaint studio next to a Christian Science Reading Room. She spends many hours there each day, working rapidly, almost urgently, to create uniquely individual interpretations of the female figure. This is Doris Caesar, a great contemporary artist and a phenomenon of our times, a woman who has succeeded as a sculptor, more than she could ever have imagined, by bringing to this timeless art her knowledge of a woman's sensitivity and a creativeness which exceeds her femininity.

In an art world where constant, almost unreasoned, change is demanded, she has ignored fads and concentrated instead on a single theme—the female figure. Her rewards for such stubborn individuality have been gratifying. Since 1931 she has exhibited regularly in New York City galleries. Her bronzes are in 38 museums and more than 500 private collections. The Whitney Museum of American Art highlighted these accomplishments in 1959 with a retrospective entitled "Four American Expressionists" and most art critics responded with lavish praise. One of them, Emory Lewis of *Cue* (January 10, 1959), considered it "a thrill to see the human form again" at a time when art exhibitions were dominated by and saturated with non-objectivity.

At first impression Doris Caesar's sculpture is a paradox, for she often creates what appear to be rather awkward-looking women with lumpy hips, aggressive breasts and limbs pulling at their sockets. But she does this in a deeply human attempt to probe into the heart of a woman's experience. By using long craning necks that culminate in pitifully small heads, she dramatizes the troubles of day-to-day living and the harsh realities of life. Yet emerging from this seeming awkwardness is an inner beauty, a kind of intuitive strength in the face of pain, and courage in the face of adversity.

Although her work is uniquely individual, one can see in it her admiration of the hauntingly romantic figures of Matthias Grünewald and Tillman Riemenschneider, the lean angular sculptures of Wilhelm Lehmbrück and the strength and expressive power of Ernst Barlach. "The northern artists mean much to me," she once wrote, "not only for their austerity, but also for their integrity and fierce emotion. I don't really believe the North Gothic tradition in art has influenced my sculpture, rather I have a feeling that the artists who represented it had great strength and were not afraid."

Other artists may not have had any direct influence on her work as she claims, but critics tend to disagree. The solitary, rather elusive silhouettes of her figures remind them of Alberto Giacometti; the exaggerated rippling surfaces of her bronzes echo Emile Antoine Bourdelle, and her simplification of form reflects the teachings of Alexander Archipenko.

Perhaps the key to a description of her mature work lies in the impression of reality her figures convey in spite of their distortions. Each bronze woman has a reason for being. Some are tender, others are tragic, but most are sad and fearful because that is part of Doris Caesar's own being.

John I.H. Baur, of the Whitney Museum of American Art, sees in them a compelling sense of life. "They are stamped with individuality, with the recognizable difference between old and young flesh, between the structure of one shoulder and another, the weight of a particular breast or hip. They are entirely believable," he writes, "in their mixture of awkwardness and grace. There is nothing in them of the heroic, nothing of the sculptured goddess. They speak in spontaneous gestures, tempered by an odd self-consciousness, an evident awareness of their bodies and what they tell of a woman's inner life. If the revelation is nearly painful in its intimacy, it is also a deeply compassionate expression of the essence of womanhood."[1]

Doris Caesar was born in Brooklyn, New York, on November 8, 1892, in a comfortable old brownstone house at 55 Willow Street where she spent her early childhood. Her mother,

Lillian Dean Porter, was a beautiful yet fragile woman whose life seemed tinged by sadness. When Doris was eleven, her mother fell gravely ill with pneumonia. A physician thought warm sunshine might help, so the family hurried to Florida in a vain effort to save her, but she never recovered. Lillian Porter was thirty-seven years old when she died.

"I'll never forget those weeks and the blow my father had to bear," she recalled. "My mother was lovely to look at, with soft wavy hair, large green eyes and a slim lovely figure. She painted, wrote poetry and helped me with my school work. She was very tender and sad, but oh so brave, and she knew, of course, that she was dying. To this day I think of her with gratitude, rather than sorrow. From that time on I realized her great strength of personal enclosure and I have never forgotten it."

The tragic loss of a mother brought the youngster closer to her father, Alfred Haynes Porter, a brilliant young lawyer who later became president of the Royal Baking Powder Company. She was fortunate indeed to have his guidance, for he had a remarkably adventurous spirit and an inquiring mind. His interests ranged from hunting dogs, golf, sailing and a fondness for driving early motor cars, to music, painting, literature, and travel. Of all things, he loved the opera best.

Alfred Porter would frequently take his daughter to the theater. They would see a performance of Richard Wagner's work at the Metropolitan Opera or, perhaps, Ethel Jackson at the New Amsterdam Theater in Franz Lehar's "The Merry Widow," and Doris would write on her program: "Seen with daddy, November 9, 1907. I liked the play." Usually they would stay for one act, then go for a walk or step into a

MÄDCHEN.
1958. Brass. 72 high.

museum to look at only one painting. In this way Mr. Porter tried hard to develop his daughter's interests and make her happy.

A move to 116 East 38th Street in New York City and extensive travel during the next seven years had a healthy effect on them. Three Mediterranean cruises enabled Doris to roam about Italy, Austria, Spain, England, Greece and Egypt, and see at first hand the treasures of Europe and Africa. There was also a trip into remote areas of the American West when much of it was little more than a wilderness. These experiences opened up a whole new world to her at a very impressionable age and they had a marked influence on her later work. "What wonderful memories go through my mind," she wrote, "everytime I read a book or go to the theater."

It is difficult to understand what motivates a girl of sixteen to want to become an artist, a career not yet respectable in 1909 for someone from Miss Chapin's fashionable girls' school. Perhaps it was the natural culmination of her experiences, or it might have been an inborn precociousness inherited from two talented parents. Whatever the reason, Alfred Porter understood, and permitted his daughter to enter the Art Students League in the fall of 1909, while she was still a morning student at the Spence School.

It was exciting. "I felt practically a bohemian," she recalled. At one o'clock each afternoon she hurried to the League to meet her new friends in the cafeteria and then spend hours talking about art, politics and life.

She stayed at the League for about four years, studying drawing under Frederic A. Bridgman and painting under several others whose names were soon forgotten. She remembered Bridgman as an artist who could draw a woman in ten minutes, but it was a woman and not a drawing. "I suppose I did get something from Bridgman and the other rather pedestrian instructors," she said, and she undoubtedly did. Unhappily it took her a long time to forget them and be herself. It was fortunate indeed, in view of this situation, that she did not study sculpture at that time.

Marriage, on December 27, 1913, to Harry Caesar, a young Princeton graduate, changed all this. There followed a period of "fun and fantasy" when no time could be spared for art.

Life moved swiftly. Two boys, Henry and Porter Caesar, were born in 1914 and 1916 as America raced headlong into World War I. A mood of exaltation gripped the country. It became a war to end wars, a war to make the world safe for democracy and, as such, it was almost a holy crusade to some people. Harry Caesar was one of them. He enlisted immediately and served overseas until the fighting stopped. But with peace came disillusionment. People were tired of foreign entanglements and were more concerned with problems at home.

The "Roaring Twenties" saw a new status for women, prohibition, the gospel of Sigmund Freud, gin, cigarettes and all-night automobile rides. "It was too gay, too heady," Doris Caesar wrote. There was too much money, bridge playing and night clubs, a hollow existence—depressing and upsetting. She badly needed a change, but summers in Rumson, New Jersey, and Leslie, a baby daughter born in 1923, failed to give her spirits a much-needed lift. On top of this, her father died the following year, "an incredible loss," and she was stricken with a brief illness. While she was recovering, her thoughts turned once more to art. "Perhaps modern art? Sculpture certainly—new, hard, something to grasp—not painting."

BALLET, no. 5.
1962. Bronze. 10 high.

Not long after that, she enrolled in Alexander Archipenko's School on 57th Street. She attended his school for five years, working almost every day from morning until night. Three-dimensional form proved to be so intriguing that it became somewhat of an obsession with her. This was hard on her family, to be sure, but Harry Caesar was wonderful about it. "He never failed me," she wrote. "In fact he got so interested in painting and sculpture that we spent all of our spare time going to museums and art galleries!" Whenever she needed him, he would be at her side, even after his father died and Harry became a very busy senior partner in the banking firm of H. A. Caesar and Company.

Archipenko was a good teacher, patient yet strong, and he gave Doris Caesar a sound knowledge of the techniques and meaning of sculpture. More important, perhaps, he possessed the remarkable ability of bringing out originality in students without influencing their direction with his own personal style.

Life was new and different—hard work, cafeterias, lunch with other students, picnics in the park and talk of art. But Archipenko's studio was too crowded, so she and two other hopeful sculptors, Sybil Kennedy and Barbara Dunbar, rented a loft on Lexington Avenue where they began the laborious task of rearranging what they had absorbed into something entirely their own. With this change, sculpture became of primary importance to Doris Caesar, and yet her mature style evolved slowly and not without some indecisiveness.

Practically nothing remains of the sculpture done by Mrs. Caesar during the late 1920's and early 1930's. But this is not unfortunate because most of it was undistinguished. Her constant use of a live model, her studied poses, coupled with a certain lack of imagination, betrayed a beginner's uncertainties and there was little to separate if from the heavy traditional female nudes being produced then.

Gradually, Mrs. Caesar's work began to show potential. Her figures were strongly modeled; they became anatomically sound, and infused with a strength and vigor that was some- what reminiscent of Rodin. Years later John I.H. Baur saw in this early work an "undoubted power . . . felt principally in their insistent physical presence, heavy, sometimes quite sensual, and little illumined by the inward quality which was to transform her later work from sculptured flesh to sculp- tured humanity."[5]

She was not discouraged by the slowness of her progress and continued to struggle for success with an enthusiasm which seemed at times to be a compulsion.

Like most aspiring artists, she was eager to exhibit, so in 1927 she had her first bronze cast, a portrait of a ten-year-old Negro boy named "Hookey." With a beginner's earnestness, she took the piece under her arm to Erhard Weyhe's book- shop and art gallery at 794 Lexington Avenue. Weyhe not only liked the attractive young woman's spirit; he was in- terested in her work and agreed to handle it. "Bring me more," he said, "I'll keep your things in the window."[3] Thus began a friendship of over forty years.

Weyhe had an infectious eagerness in his Teutonic make-up that was tremendously inspiring. They talked about art and he introduced her to contemporary German and English sculpture that he was fond of collecting. She spent hours at the gallery, studying sculpture by Barlach, Lehmbrück and Rudolf Belling, paintings by Emil Nolde, and the prints of Kathe Kollwitz.

Erhard Weyne

SLEEPING PAIR.
1934. Bronze. 10 high.

The work of French artists such as Aristide Maillol and Emile-Antoine Bourdelle was less attractive, but she dearly loved to browse through Daumier's lithographs, something that is reflected in her work of the mid-1930's.

Oddly enough, she did not have her first one-man exhibition at Weyhe's, for Carl Zigrosser, who managed the gallery, insisted that she was not yet ready. "Of course Zigrosser was right," she later admitted. "But Mr. Weyhe encouraged me."

In spite of Zigrosser's warnings, she persuaded the Montross Gallery to show her work in 1931, only to be soundly condemned by critics for over-emphasizing portrait heads. After seeing a particularly biting review, Alexander Archipenko sent Doris Caesar a warm note of encouragement. "Do not be disappointed at the stupidity of this art critic," he wrote. "Please read in the same magazine what was said about Matisse and you will see that art is not for everybody. I am sure that in your artistic career you will be surprised many times at the dumbness of some art critics."[4]

Two years later Montross exhibited her work again; this time some critics were impressed. According to Edward Alden Jewell of *The New York Times* (April 23, 1933), those who saw the first show might find themselves unprepared for the "large imaginatively conceived, [and] triumphantly released figures" by "this gifted sculptor."

The *Brooklyn Eagle* (April 16, 1933) called them "strikingly different," while the *New York American* (April 22, 1933) reluctantly termed her improvement "superficial," since her work left "much to be desired, being excited, hothearted and insufficiently restrained."

At about this time Mr. Weyhe introduced her to Rudolf Belling, the great German sculptor, who had just arrived in New

York. They talked for several hours, leaning on the book shelves at Weyhe's. Belling was attracted by what she had done, the spaces, distortions, nuances that leaned toward abstractions, so she studied with him between 1934 and 1936. Mrs. Caesar later recalled, "He had a terrific impact on me— a nervous harried person but profoundly stimulating." Belling was a good influence; he was dynamic and sure, possessed with an almost ruthless strength, and he taught her to think in a disciplined "German way."

Some days, when work went poorly, she would leave her studio in the Sherwood Building, visit galleries or stop to see other artists, talking sculpture—"long exciting talks," perhaps with someone like Joseph Brummer. He was a huge man with a strong German accent, giving an impression of power—a sort of spiritual power—and he was helpful and interested in her sculpture.

Doris Caesar had long felt doubts about her preoccupation with the human and emotional quality of her work. Contact with Belling stimulated her to experiment with abstractions, and for about a year so-called "pure forms" in wood were at the heart of her work.

But she lost interest in this medium and soon became convinced that she could not possibly express herself satisfactorily with "pure forms." After destroying most of these mediocre sculptures, something she did periodically throughout her career, Doris Caesar returned once more to modeling people.

Her experimentation continued, however, this time without any sharp departure from the intensely expressive figures and heads that were typical of her work. There were radical elongations of the body in which thinness was carried to extremes, even to stick-like proportions on occasion, but the results were far from satisfying because they seemed to lack any deep conviction. Yet out of this came an understanding of how difficult different techniques could be, a knowledge that would be of inestimable value in the future.

It wasn't until 1935 that Weyhe finally gave her an exhibition. The results were more encouraging than ever because she had begun to show signs of the personal style for which her work would soon become famous. In reviewing the exhibition, the *New York Herald Tribune* hinted at future success: "This artist shows herself more of a realist than an imaginative or creative type; but there is grace and feeling in her work, and she has an excellent technical foundation as a basis for future achievements."

She frequently turned to poetry during these years as another means of expressing her artistic impressions, for it had always been important to her creativity. Being a poor sleeper, she would awaken at midnight and read until dawn, or get up at 5 a.m., light a fire, curl up in a chair, and write for two or three hours. "I loved the night hours," she recalled, "so quiet and peaceful," and she devoted herself to poetry, reading widely, but especially T.S. Eliot, the Sitwells, Walt Whitman and W.H. Auden.

The Poetry Review accepted some poems; then G.P. Putnam's simultaneously published two volumes entitled *Phantom Thoughts* and *Certain Paths*. They were not successful, but they were sensitive individual poetic expressions, vivid in imagery, revealing the longings of a groping, rather unsatisfied person.

"I hold my breath in very ecstasy at life's beauty," she wrote in one of these poems, referring to the splendor a human

THE DOCTOR.
1937. Bronze.

being feels rather than senses, the beauty that lies within a person's sensitivity, not just on the surface.[5] She sought to express this in the momentary mood of her subjects of the 1930's by leaving her surfaces rough and spontaneous looking, perhaps showing a mother tenderly holding a sick child or a woman locked deep in silent thought. These scenes were recorded, not with a photographer's eye, but with a poet's sympathy, giving form to the feeling aroused within her heart.

Doris Caesar worked rapidly then, as always, in an effort to transmit, by sheer nervous energy, her own emotional excitement into the small clay figures taking shape in her hands. It is almost as if she were driven by a fear that her figures might not be fully alive, or thoroughly infused with an inner emotional feeling. They gave the impression that she often selected her subjects on the run and modeled them in much the same way.

Howard Devree emphasized this in the *Magazine of Art* (April, 1937) when he wrote: "She can and does get amazing volume into a little bronze torso—but she remains a romantic realist with a predisposition toward putting action into her composition."

The spontaneous quality of the artist's sketch-like sculptures in the 1930's was somewhat akin to Daumier and Kollwitz, but without the social implications they sought to convey. One of the better sculptures of this period, "The Doctor," was typical of those early years, having been drawn from the pattern of common life. In it she depicted two rather homely middle-aged people awaiting a diagnosis from a doctor who was just making a house call. Although the style of "The Doctor" did not differ appreciably from what she had been doing, it had a deep sense of warmth, humor and sadness, showing that Doris Caesar had matured toward what would one day become her main strength as a sculptor.

Her notes on life in the late 1930's recall a Barlach exhibition at Westermans in 1937. "Also that year Curt Valentin's show at 3 West 46 of Lehmbruck; everything lent by Mr. Weyhe— terribly exciting show . . . The World's Fair in 1939—had my large 'Mother and Child' in American section. Some of the people of those years . . . Saul Baizerman, Diego Rivera, Roaul Hague, Chaim Gross, Hugo Robus, Minna Harkavy— a mess of a show of course, but exhilarating."[6]

About 1940, Mrs. Caesar appeared to regress slightly in her work when she created a series of large clothed figures in an effort to obtain greater solidity. This may have been a reaction to earlier experiments with elongations. But whatever her reasons for this change, these figures proved to be too traditional and about the most uninteresting of her career. Yet, surprising as it may seem, critics in general praised them.

Margaret Breuning of the New York *Journal-American* (February 25, 1940), viewed them as a "logical growth toward a fuller expression . . . ." In *The New York Times* (February 25, 1940), Edward Alden Jewell said that he liked the notable simplicity of a slightly over-life-sized group titled "Unity" (a man, woman and child), and *Cue* (March 2, 1940), saw these sculptures as "brilliantly rhythmic . . . with taste and understanding."

World War II brought about sharp changes and many responsibilities for Mrs. Caesar. "Harry deeply involved in Dogs for Defense; boys away, two children married . . .," she wrote in her notes. "Leaves and goodbyes, babies living with us— mothers following camps; death of my step-mother—her

ST. FRANCIS RECEIVING THE STIGMATA.
1958. Bronze. 22 high. Collections of Brooks Memorial Gallery,
Memphis, Tennessee and St. John's Abbey, Collegeville, Minnesota.

youngest became mine—lived with us (20 years old), husband away—more babies."[7] Although it was a difficult and worrisome period for her, she somehow managed to find time to work on new sculpture.

After Weyhe closed his gallery during the war Curt Valentin handled her sculpture. He was a strange shy man, prone to a little too much drinking, but an expert judge of sculpture. Twice a year until his death Valentin visited Mrs. Caesar's studio to discuss and criticize her work. And in 1943 he gave her a one-man exhibition, a truly inspirational show, from which her first sculpture was purchased by a museum.

Throughout the 1940's the artist's mature style showed signs of evolving into a character entirely its own. This was not an abrupt change, to be sure, for her "St. Francis" of 1947 still reflected considerable admiration for El Greco, whose work she had seen while in Spain several years before. But it was a passionate "St. Francis," truly her own, with gaunt hands stretching heavenward to receive the stigmata—the wounds of Christ.

The same thing can be said about her "Mother and Child" of 1947, which still showed the artist's admiration for Barlach. It was a portrait of Doris Caesar's daughter Leslie holding her third child, a self-contained sculpture filled with a sense of dignity and fused with tenderness and deep emotion. Of course Leslie did not pose for it. She did not have to. It just came.

John I. H. Baur stressed the significance of this piece when he wrote: "The 'Mother and Child' . . . points the direction of her ultimate development and is, in itself, a work of sensitivity. The theme, so easily reduced to bathos, has here a deep tenderness combined with almost impersonal

MOTHER AND CHILD.
1947. Bronze. 13 high.

strength." He emphasized that the modeling was "subtly varied, catching the strain of the hand, building the brooding, long contours of the head and playing with lightness over the sleeping child. If the piece is more traditional and less exciting in a formal sense than her later works, it still has the authority of emotion plastically expressed."[8]

Caesar's intense dedication to sculpture was more pronounced after the war. There was the "Wonder of peace and getting old," she recalled, "the freedom of maturity and age," and she became so completely absorbed by her sculpture career that she would often work fifteen to twenty hours a day, sometimes hardly sleeping at all.

Sureness in handling surface and form, a firmer perception of the relation of distortion to subject matter, and the discipline to execute an idea effectively were her rewards for such dedication. More than anything else, her development appears to have been one of refinement and a deeper compassion for a disheartened human race.

Gradually the elongation of her figures grew more pronounced, sometimes reaching toward abstraction without any loss of grace or strength. The hands were far more expressive than they had ever been. Often they were eloquent, even poignant, telling a story as forcefully as a facial expression might do.

Throughout these years the artist's activities in the art world kept her terribly busy. There were Sunday forums in Greenwich Village, the New School for Social Research, conversations with Fred Buchholz, John Sloan and others, a vice presidency of the Board of the National Association of Women Artists and membership on the Board of the New York Society of Women Artists.

In 1948, she joined "The New York Six," a group of sculptors, all members of the National Association of Women Artists, who joined together for a group show at the Argent Galleries. Besides Doris Caesar there were Rhys Caparn, Minna Harkavy, Helen Phillips, Helena Simkhovitch and Arline Wingate. Although their styles differed considerably, ranging from classic portraiture to bold abstractions, they shared one thing in common—a preference to model their work rather than chiseling or carving it.

The successful New York exhibition of "The Six" attracted the attention of André Chamson, director of the Petit Palais in Paris, who invited them to exhibit in Paris to provide "a bridge of understanding between artists and art lovers on both sides of the ocean." Twelve to fifteen pieces were shown by each sculptor at the exhibition. Attendance totaled in the thousands, and it was a great success. Just as important—the reviews were good.

That same year the Caesars built a country house at Salem Center, about fifty miles north of New York City. It was built high on a boulder-strewn hillside overlooking a distant lake, with a studio attached. Being a city girl she did not know whether such isolation would work, but it did.

They spent weekends there at first, since the village was nothing more than one store and a few houses. Weekdays in New York were filled with work, shows and friends. Yet she found a certain tranquility in the country, something unknown to her in the past, and could work better there, so the Caesars moved permanently into the country. It was a wise decision. Complete concentration and solitude became a way of life.

With all this there was a sudden coming of age, a surprisingly radical change for the better. In the early 1950's she

51

abandoned her story-telling technique, the use of a male figure, portraiture, and largely eliminated facial expressions on her figures, which by then were exclusively women. In a large part this was due to the influence of Curt Valentine. "Now," he said, "you are ready to be a sculptor." [9]

Since 1951, the theme of most of her sculpture has been limited to the female nude. That year she created a life-sized nude, the first in a series for which she has become famous. One might wonder how an artist could possibly have avoided repetition while concentrating on a single theme for so many years, and yet she has succeeded remarkably well.

Each figure is decidedly different, each has a spirit and personality of its own, perhaps because no woman is like another. With this in mind, she has drawn from her women, in a most resourceful way, an absorbing expression of what it is to be a woman, or, perhaps more simply, what it is to "be."

"I do not feel hemmed in by this self-imposed boundary," she once said. "Rather it serves as a means for deeper creative penetration [since] there is no creature more complex than women." Then, with a faint smile on her lips, she added: "I know because I am a woman."

The heads of her figures grew smaller and somewhat mask-like, possibly to suggest primitive African characteristics and as a means of giving each sculpture a universal quality. Above all else, she wanted them to have bodies that were symbolic of the flesh and blood of all women, strong, even cold, with a sense of enclosure—the essence of womanhood.

With maturity came strength, the power to build bone and muscle without relying on patches of unsmoothed clay or thumb and spatula marks for effect. "The flesh has a virginal tautness," declared John I.H. Baur, "it is weighted by the ripeness of maturity, it is hacked and furrowed, hollowed and bossed by childbirth, by desire, by submission and the stresses of experience."[10]

That was not all. Baur saw in the modeling a quality entirely its own. "It moves with independent rhythms, slow and fast, light and heavy. There is an electric quality in the surface, a tensity, a vitality which is apart, again, from the physical vitality of the figure itself, though inevitably contributing to it. The rhythms are not obvious ones of contour and volume, not the flowing edges and composed shapes which the classical artist uses. They consist, rather, in plays of light and shadow, of rough and smooth, of strong motions abruptly stopped, or turned back upon themselves or subsiding in relaxed passages, to break out again elsewhere."[11]

She has never permitted virtuosity to be better than an idea. If a sculpture turns out to be too pretty or too decorative, it is taken apart because she is not interested in prettiness. It is what is inside that matters.

This, according to Baur, "is romantic sculpture in the baroque tradition, but without the baroque's theatricality. It is built on change [and] motion . . . but it speaks with a modern voice which distrusts the grand gesture and tempers romanticism with a deep sense of reality."[12]

Many years before this, Doris Caesar stopped using live models to break away from reality and capture a certain freshness in her work. When beginning a new piece she often asks herself: "Well, what shall I do today?" After pondering the question, she gathers some wire and clay together and sets up a strong, pliable armature that has flexibility blended with a minimum of tension. Having reached this point, she walks around the framework, twisting the

REPOSE.
1966. Bronze. 12 high.

wires to balance them properly, at the same time wondering just what to make. Finally, she begins putting on clay.

From this moment, everything goes smoothly unless her feelings or the problems involved with the piece are not well ahead of her technical ability. Sometimes this is a difficult thing to recognize, but if there are doubts, she pauses for a while, sometimes not returning to sculpture for a month.

When working, Doris Caesar is in a world of her own, completely detached, treasuring the loneliness that makes an individual a self-contained personality. She loves the inwardness of a contemplative life.

But when the clay model is completed, an assistant is called in to help prepare molds for casting the piece at the Modern Art Foundry in New York. She spends considerable time at the foundry to be certain that each bronze is finished in the correct texture and color. This is usually done with the aid of John and Bob Spring, two experts who handle this rather exacting work.

One of her most outstanding sculptures was inspired by Curt Valentin in 1953, when he telephoned to ask if it would be all right to visit Salem Center that weekend to explore the possibility of a one-man exhibition at his gallery. That was qualified, of course, with "if Mr. Weyhe approved." Doris Caesar was pleased because she had been hard at work for a month on three large figures, her first over-life-sized women, and she had also been thinking of a really large torso. Valentin's call encouraged her to try the torso, even though only five days remained until his expected arrival.

Working quickly, in a super-human effort to please her master critic, she succeeded in finishing it before Valentin reached Salem Center. He was delighted with it and asked to have one cast for the proposed show, along with every new figure in her studio. These plans never materialized, unfortunately, for he suffered a fatal heart attack in Italy several months later. This major work was later acquired by the Whitney Museum for its permanent collection.

The 1950's were good years for Doris Caesar. There were ten successful one-man shows, culminating in 1959 with an exhibition assembled by the Whitney, featuring, in addition to Mrs. Caesar, Chaim Gross, Karl Knaths and Abraham Rattner.

Of the one-man shows, the twenty-five-year retrospective at Weyhe's Gallery in 1957 must be considered the most notable. All of the sculptures were lent by collectors and museums especially for the exhibition and the critics unanimously praised it. Reporting for *The New York Times* (October 17, 1957), Howard Devree described her development well when he wrote: "Integrity and a very personal approach have always characterized the sculpture of Doris Caesar . . . . Her work is modern with respect for tradition and she has worked consistently with the human figure without being led down blind alleys or into 'isms' or the quest of novelty,"

At about this time, John I. H. Baur talked with the artist about an exhibition the Whitney had under consideration. He wanted to include her work in it in a kind of retrospective. This was quite encouraging news, although two years were to pass before the exhibition became a reality. But when the "Four American Expressionists" show opened, it was a tremendous success.

"A really beautiful exhibition, presented with a flair and sensitivity," she confided in her notes, "thirty pieces covering a span of thirty years. Wonderfully presented against white walls. The catalogue for the show was superb—written by Jack Baur, a brilliant man. What a wonderful and magnificent thing to happen. People flocked in. Had show at Weyhe's at the same time—terrific success. The Whitney is filled with wonderful people." [13]

Once again the critics reacted favorably. Bennett Schiff of the *New York Post* (January 23, 1959), saw her sculpture as "a continuing exploration of the expressiveness of the nude female body, modeled with great skill in clay and cast in bronze. Her search is for essence of womanhood . . . . It is a subject which she handles with sensitive feeling," he said, "distorting freely and with intensity, bending, building, stretching and manipulating the fundamental form in order to say what she sees in womanhood." And Rual Askew of *The Dallas Morning News* (December 6, 1959), pointed out that she was "one of the few women ever ranked at the top of her art . . . ," and thanked her for intensifying the public's "awareness of what it is simply to be."

For Doris Caesar it was a great and inspiring decade, with the Whitney exhibition "the icing" on her "sculpture cake," and she was grateful for every minute of it.

In Salem Center, and then in Litchfield, Connecticut, where the Caesars moved in 1957, there had come a magnificent flowering in her work which established her as a leading American sculptor.

She was now 66 years old, an age when most people are worn out, but not Doris Caesar. She continued to amaze everyone by the fierceness with which she approached her sculpture. "I never cease to marvel at your extraordinary creative energy," wrote John Baur, "and the consistent quality of all your work." [14] Indeed, work had become an in-

ST. JOHN THE BAPTIST.
1961. Bronze. 84 high. Collection of St. John's Abbey,
Collegeville, Minnesota.

tegral part of the artist's make-up, and in 1960 she appeared stronger than at any time in her life. Of course, her style had changed over the years—the elongations, her own idiom of expression, and her sculpture had become more sophisticated and knowing, but, at the same time, she found it impossible to deepen the feeling for humanity she had captured so well many years before.

"I think I have more awareness now, but the sorrows and difficulties of life seem a little less important," she wrote. "My thinking runs now in the direction of strength. It is the strength in people that moves me. The wonderful power to handle and accept, or, if not to accept, to beat." [15]

During the late 1950's and early 1960's several innovations appeared in her work—flowers and religious figures—although women continued to be her primary interest.

The flowers were really orchid plants, inspired, no doubt, by the Caesars' greenhouse, which was filled with them. The results were disappointing, however, because the orchids seemed too heavy and rigid in bronze. Worst of all, they had a mysterious anthropomorphic quality, as if the dark blossoms and leaves were actually arms or fingers reaching out, almost pleading with the beholder.

Her religious figures, on the contrary, were surprisingly successful even though most contemporary artists tend to treat such subjects as somewhat of an anathema. Although she had done several of them in the past, a strong impetus to do more came from St. John's College at Collegeville, Minnesota, where the noted architect, Marcel Breuer, created a beautiful modernistic church. Through Breuer's influence, the Benedictine officials commissioned Doris Caesar to do a seven-foot statue of "St. John the Baptist."

ANNUNCIATION.
1960. Bronze. 78 high. Collection of St. John's Abbey,
Collegeville, Minnesota.

60

This proved to be a great challenge. Some of the monks thought the completed plaster too modern after seeing photographs of it and questioned its appropriateness as a means of expressing the faith of their ancient order. When an impasse developed, the Right Reverend Baldwin Dworschak, the head of St. John's College, flew to New York to see the sculpture. Accompanied by the artist and Marcel Breuer, the Abbot visited the hot, clanging foundry to confront the plaster-white, angry-looking figure of St. John.

Naturally, he was hesitant, much to Mrs. Caesar's discomfort, for it really wasn't what he expected. He thought the mouth of this rather monstrous white figure too prominent, the eyes too deep, and the neck muscles too rugged. Sensing that the Abbot could not quite visualize what "St. John" would look like in bronze, the artist begged him not to insist on any changes.

After deliberating for some time, Abbot Dworschak finally turned to Mrs. Caesar and Breuer, thought for a few seconds more, and said: "Well, I'm a little afraid, but I will trust the judgment of you two." [16]

When the Abbot saw the finished bronze, however, he agreed whole-heartedly and ordered five more sculptures, including "Annunciation," considered by the artist to be one of her finest works. Two of these sculptures were eventually exhibited in the Vatican Pavilion during the 1964 New York World's Fair.

"St. Benedict," commissioned in 1965, by St. Gregory's Priory in Three Rivers, Michigan, proved to be even more of a problem when Doris Caesar inadvertently dressed the Episcopal monk in Franciscan robes. The error may have shaken her patrons' confidence in her ability, for they complained that "St. Benedict's" waist seemed a little too feminine and his lower lip too sensual.

Despite her rather embarrassing mistake, these complaints brought forth Doris Caesar's determination. "I do not consider the lower lip too sensual," she replied. "On the contrary, I would call it somewhat aggressive—which was just what I wanted to express." As for the plaster, she felt that it was necessary to work in this way when aiming towards bronze. While admitting that the plaster did look somewhat extreme, perhaps even frighteningly so, she assured the Father Prior that the bronze would absorb this harsh look.[17]

She then told Father Prior Benedict Reid not to be discouraged with the photographs and cited Benvenuto Cellini, who said: "Clay is the life, plaster the death and bronze the resurrection." Then she strongly suggested that it would not do to change "St. Benedict" because she felt it would be a powerful figure, one which avoided the look of a man, while retaining an idea of dedication.[18]

Changing the robes took about a month, but the results were good. When the Prior saw the bronze, he wrote: "Now we can see the resurrection."

Events moved rapidly in the 1960's. Erhard Weyhe's health declined, so Gertrude Dennis, his wonderfully capable daughter, took over management of the gallery. Doris Caesar's work changed too. Perhaps the religious figures loosened her style a little, for her women appeared stronger, more meaningful, and more imaginative.

In commenting on her work of the 1960's for *The New York Times* (February 22, 1964), Brian O'Doherty wrote that they survived better esthetically than one might expect. "Some became quite expressive after a while, replacing a first impression of strain and arbitrariness." Three years later *Time* magazine (April 7, 1967), said "Caesar's women still manage to stand very tall." Indeed, they stood very tall, and a new feeling of authority seemed to have crept into them, a feeling of coldness and sureness, with less emotion, perhaps stemming from her hardened determination to be herself.

Although Doris Caesar's work has changed radically through the years, her female subjects have changed little. In texture and quality they are a continuation of her earlier work, and yet they suggest endless new possibilities, perhaps because no woman is like another. Each is enclosed within her body and each is symbolic of womanhood. Caesar's women possess a sense of life—all life. They are the inner image of all women; not graceful, but flawed and graceless, with a sense of anonymity. As such, their worn and distorted figures force us to recognize, with understanding and perhaps affection, every woman's awkward humanness.

All quotations are from conversations with the artist unless otherwise noted.

64

THE WIDOW.
1948. Bronze. 74 high.
Collections of the Syracuse University
Museum of Art, Syracuse, New York
and the Philadelphia Museum
of Art, Philadelphia, Pennsylvania.

Detail (left)

BALLET, no. 6.
1965. Bronze. 11 high.

SEATED WOMAN.
1967. Bronze. 20 high.

KNEELING WOMAN.
1958. Bronze. 60 high. Collection of the Syracuse University
Museum of Art, Syracuse, New York.

Detail (right)

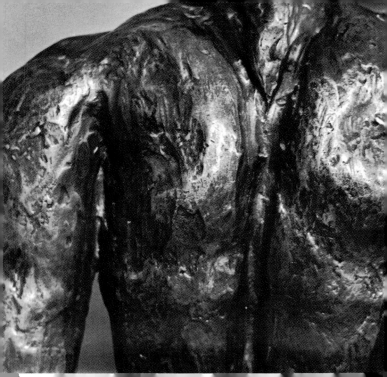

STANDING WOMAN, arm across eyes.
1964. Brass. 14 high.

A STATUE stood
And calmly faced the crowded room.
I looked and saw
Its steady eyes
Fixed with cold rigidity
On space.
And felt with my hand
The cool hard surface
Of motionless muscles—
Here was a mood,
Caught and held in static poise,
And as I looked
I knew, that mood
And moment
Would go on and on,
When all of us that looked
Would change and weary and forget.

Doris Caesar

STANDING WOMAN. (right)
1957. Bronze. 72 high. Collection of the Syracuse University
Museum of Art, Syracuse, New York.

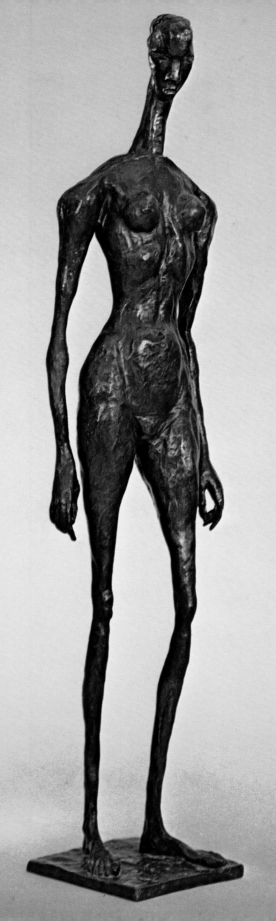

73

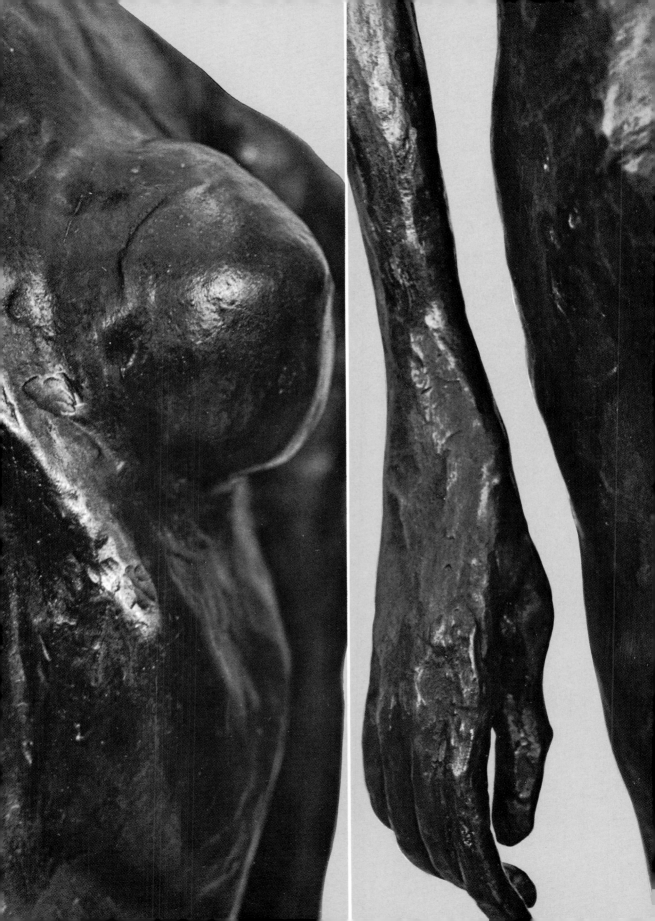

RAPTURE.
1963. Bronze. 17 high.

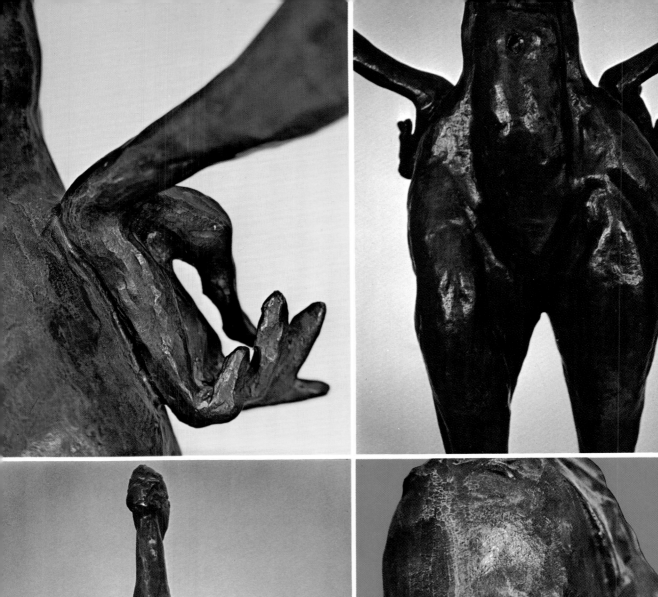

STANDING WOMAN, hands on hips.
1951. Bronze. 76 high.
Collection of the Syracuse University
Museum of Art, Syracuse, New York.

Details (left)

RELEASE.
1959. Bronze. 33 high.

BALANCE.
1962. Bronze. 15 high.

CRUCIFIX. (left)
1967. Bronze. 82 high. Collection of the Syracuse University
Museum of Art, Syracuse, New York.

ELLIPSE.
1962. Brass. 11 high.

SLEEPWALKER.
1968. Bronze. 29 high.

CHRONOLOGY

1892   Born November 8 in Brooklyn, New York.

1909-1913   Studied drawing and painting at the Art Students League under Frederic A. Bridgman.

1913   Married Harry A. Caesar on December 27.

1925   Entered Alexander Archipenko's art school to study sculpture.

1927   Cast first bronze, a portrait titled: "Hookey."

1931   First one-man exhibition at the Montross Gallery.

1934   Two books of her poems published by G. P. Putnam's entitled: *Phantom Thoughts* and *Certain Paths.*

1934-1935   Studied sculpture with Rudolf Belling.

1935   First major exhibition at the Weyhe Gallery.

1943   Curt Valentin gave her a one-man exhibition at the Buchholz Gallery.

1949   Exhibited with "The New York Six" at the Petit Palais in Paris.

1953   Abandoned earlier themes as subjects to concentrate almost exclusively on women.

1957   Twenty-five year retrospective at Weyhe's acclaimed by critics.

1959   Retrospective at Whitney Museum of American Art as part of "Four American Expressionists" exhibition.

1960-1969   Series of one-man exhibitions at Weyhe's.

1969   Awarded Honorary Doctorate of Fine Arts Degree at Syracuse University.

TWO WOMEN.
1961. Bronze. 32 high.

SEATED WOMAN, head on knees.
1961. Bronze. 5 high.

HEAD.
1964. Bronze. 10 high.

MEMORY, no. 2.
1961. Bronze. 30 high.

ONE-MAN EXHIBITIONS

1969   Weyhe Gallery, New York, New York.

1968   Weyhe Gallery, New York, New York.

1967   Weyhe Gallery, New York, New York.

1964   Weyhe Gallery, New York, New York.

1963   Richelle Gallery, St. Louis, Missouri.

1961   Sharon Creative Arts Foundation Gallery, Sharon, Connecticut.

        Weyhe Gallery, New York, New York.

1960   Wadsworth Atheneum, Hartford, Connecticut.

1959   "Four American Expressionists," Whitney Museum of American Art, New York, New York.

        "Four American Expressionists," Colorado Springs Fine Arts Center, Colorado Springs, Colorado.

        "Four American Expressionists," Columbus Gallery of Art, Columbus, Ohio.

        "Four American Expressionists," Currier Gallery of Art, Manchester, New Hampshire.

        "Four American Expressionists," Dallas Museum of Fine Arts, Dallas, Texas.

        Weyhe Gallery, New York, New York.

1958   Howard University, Washington, D.C.

1957   Weyhe Gallery, New York, New York.

1956   Margaret Brown Gallery, Boston, Massachusetts.

1955   Katonah Gallery, Katonah, New York.

1953   Weyhe Gallery, New York, New York.

1947   Weyhe Gallery, New York, New York.

1943   Buchholz Gallery (Curt Valentin), New York, New York.

1940   Fifteen Gallery, New York, New York.

1939   Weyhe Gallery, New York, New York.

1937   Weyhe Gallery, New York, New York.

1935   Weyhe Gallery, New York, New York.

1933   Montross Gallery, New York, New York.

1932   Crillon Galleries, Philadelphia, Pennsylvania.

1931   Montross Gallery, New York, New York.

ST. ANTHONY OF THE DESERT.
1961. Bronze. 60 high. Collection of St. John's Abbey,
Collegeville, Minnesota.

WOMAN IN SKIRT.
1961. Bronze. 55 high.

GROUP EXHIBITIONS

1968   New Haven Summer Festival, New Haven, Connecticut.

1967   Mattatuck Museum, Waterbury, Connecticut.

1966   Prima Mostra Internazionale d'Arte Sacra, Trieste, Italy.

Sculptors Guild Annual Exhibition, Lever House, New York, New York.

1965   "K" Gallery, Woodstock, New York.

Vatican Pavilion, New York World's Fair, New York, New York.

1964   Vatican Pavilion, New York World's Fair, New York, New York.

1963   Art Festival, West Hartford, Connecticut.

Esposizione Internazionale di Pittura e Scultura, Padua, Italy.

Federation of Modern Painters and Sculptors Annual Exhibition, Lever House, New York, New York.

Seventh Centennial Festival of St. Anthony, Padua, Italy.

1962   Norfolk Museum, Norfolk, Virginia.

Sculptors Guild Annual Exhibition, Lever House, New York, New York.

1961   Audubon Artists Annual Exhibition, National Academy Galleries, New York, New York.

Prima Mostra Internazionale d'Arte Sacra, Trieste, Italy.

Sculptors Guild Annual Exhibition, Lever House, New York, New York.

1960   Brooks Memorial Gallery, Memphis, Tennessee.

Sculptors Guild Annual Exhibition, Lever House, New York, New York.

Whitney Annual Exhibition, Whitney Museum of American Art, New York, New York.

1959   Pennsylvania Academy of the Fine Arts, Philadelphia, Pennsylvania.

Salzburg Festival of Religious Art, Salzburg, Austria.

1958   Salzburg Festival of Religious Art, Salzburg, Austria.

1957   Greenwich Gallery, New York, New York.

Whitney Annual Exhibition, Whitney Museum of American Art, New York, New York.

1956   Katonah Gallery, Katonah, New York.

Martha Jackson Gallery, New York, New York.

New Burlington Gallery, London, England.

New York Society of Women Artists Annual Exhibition, National Academy Galleries, New York, New York.

Silvermine Guild of Artists Exhibition, Stratford, Connecticut.

1955   Metropolitan Museum of Art, New York, New York.

1954   Federation of Art Traveling Exhibition.

New York Society of Women Artists Annual Exhibition, National Academy Galleries, New York, New York.

"Ten Women Artists," Riverside Museum, New York, New York.

Whitney Annual Exhibition, Whitney Museum of American Art, New York, New York.

1953   Creative Art Associates Annual Exhibition, Riverside Museum, New York, New York.

Federation of Art Traveling Exhibition.

National Association of Women Artists Annual Exhibition, National Academy Galleries, New York, New York.

Pennsylvania Academy of the Fine Arts, Philadelphia, Pennsylvania.

"Sculpture—The Tumultuous Quarter Century," Sculpture Center, New York, New York.

1952   Audubon Artists Annual Exhibition, National Academy Galleries, New York, New York.

Kalamazoo Institute of Art, Kalamazoo, Michigan.

National Association of Women Artists Annual Exhibition, National Academy Galleries, New York, New York.

New York Society of Women Artists Annual Exhibition, National Academy Galleries, New York, New York.

1951   National Association of Women Artists Annual Exhibition, Argent Galleries, New York, New York.

New York Association for the Blind Benefit Exhibition, The Lighthouse, New York, New York.

Sculptors Guild Annual Exhibition, American Museum of Natural History, New York, New York.

1950   National Association of Women Artists Annual Exhibition, Argent Galleries, New York, New York.

New York Six, Petit Palais, Paris.

New York Society of Women Artists Annual Exhibition, Demotte Gallery, New York, New York.

Sculptors Guild Annual Exhibition, Argent Galleries, New York, New York.

Whitney Annual Exhibition, Whitney Museum of American Art, New York, New York.

1949   National Association of Women Artists Annual Exhibition, Argent Galleries, New York, New York.

New York Society of Women Artists Annual Exhibition, Riverside Museum, New York, New York.

Whitney Annual Exhibition, New York, New York.

1948   National Association of Women Artists Sculpture Exhibition, Argent Galleries, New York, New York.

Whitney Annual Exhibition, Whitney Museum of American Art, New York, New York.

1947   Whitney Annual Exhibition, Whitney Museum of American Art, New York, New York.

1946   New York Society of Women Artists Annual Exhibition, Argent Galleries, New York, New York.

New York Society of Women Artists Annual Exhibition, National Academy Galleries, New York, New York.

1945   Buchholz Gallery (Curt Valentin), New York, New York.

National Association of Women Artists Annual Exhibition, National Academy Galleries, New York, New York.

New York Society of Women Artists Annual Exhibition, Riverside Museum, New York, New York.

1944   National Association of Women Artists Annual Exhibition, American Fine Arts Gallery, New York, New York.

Sculptors Guild Annual Exhibition, American British Art Center, New York, New York.

1942   Society of Independent Artists, Fine Arts Gallery, New York, New York.

Metropolitan Museum of Art, New York, New York.

"Sculpture of Freedom," Sculptors Guild Outdoor Exhibition, New York, New York.

Whitney Annual Exhibition, Whitney Museum of American Art, New York, New York.

1941   "American Sculpture Today," Buchholz Gallery (Curt Valentin), New York, New York.

Everhart Museum, Scranton, Pennsylvania.

Fifteen Gallery, New York, New York.

National Association of Women Artists Annual Exhibition, Fine Arts Gallery, New York, New York.

New York Society of Women Artists Annual Exhibition, Riverside Museum, New York, New York.

Utica Public Library Exhibition, Utica, New York.

1940   Argent Galleries, New York, New York.

Contemporary Arts Building, New York World's Fair, New York, New York.

Fifteen Gallery, New York, New York.

National Association of Women Artists Annual Exhibition, Fine Arts Gallery, New York, New York.

New York Society of Women Artists Annual Exhibition, Grant Studios, New York, New York.

Society of Independent Artists, Fine Arts Gallery, New York, New York.

"Sculpture International," Philadelphia Museum of Art, Philadelphia, Pennsylvania.

Whitney Annual Exhibition, Whitney Museum of American Art, New York, New York.

1939   Contemporary Arts Building, New York World's Fair, New York, New York.

Decorators Club Exhibition, New York, New York.

National Association of Women Artists Annual Exhibition, American Fine Arts Gallery, New York, New York.

New York Society of Women Artists Annual Exhibition, Riverside Museum, New York, New York.

1938   Argent Galleries, New York, New York.

Fifteen Gallery, New York, New York.

National Association of Women Artists Annual Exhibition, American Fine Arts Gallery, New York, New York.

SEATED WOMAN.
1962. Bronze. 6 high.

STANDING WOMAN.
1968. Bronze. 58 high.

Detail (right)

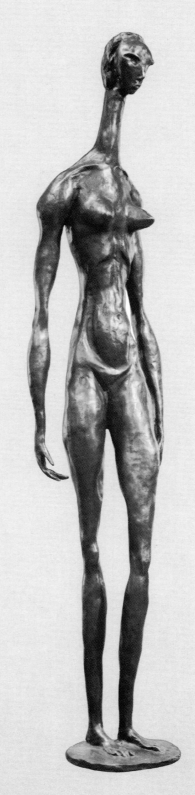

STANDING GIRL.
1968. Bronze. 33 high.

SEATED WOMAN, hands in back.
1963. Bronze. 28 high.

Study for seated woman.
c. 1940. Watercolor. 22 x 16½.

Study for clothed figure. (right)
c. 1939. Watercolor. 22 x 16½.

WINGS.
1962. Bronze. 29 high.

STANDING WOMAN, arms raised.
1958. Bronze. 18 high.

STANDING WOMAN.
1967. Bronze.10½ high.

Study for nude figures. (left)
c. 1938. Watercolor. 22 x 16½.

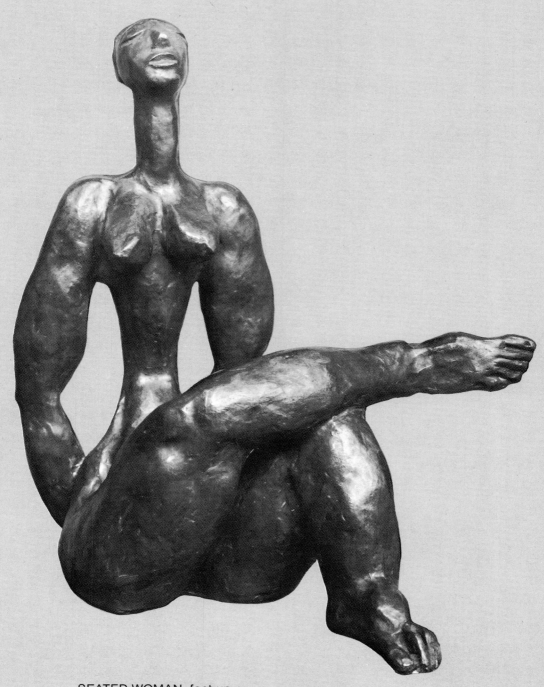

SEATED WOMAN, foot up.
1954. Bronze. 23 high. Collection of the State University
of New York, College at New Paltz, New York.

WOMAN, sitting back on heels.
1964. Bronze. 35 high.

THE pattern of my life
Is spread before me—
Lovely pattern
Run through with ugly threads,
And yet,
These threads
Pulled out
The pattern falls apart—
Smoothed down,
The nap spells courage
But rubbed
The other way
Cowardice shows—
Sunlight streams on
Truth and honesty
But in the dark
A strain stands out
Of falsehood—
But still the pattern glows,
Complete
A shining thing
A monument
To having failed
And tried again.

Doris Caesar

Study for DISPLACED PERSON. (right)
c. 1948. Watercolor. 22 x 16½.

FLEET MOMENT.
1959. Bronze. 31 high.

SEATED TORSO.
1958. Bronze. 32 high.

112

Caesar

Study for clothed figure. (left)
c. 1939. Watercolor. 22 x 16½.

DANCING FIGURE.
1959. Bronze. 10 high.

TORSO.
1955. Bronze. 45 high.

FAR EAST.
1967. Bronze. 57 high. Wustum Museum of Fine Arts,
Racine, Wisconsin.

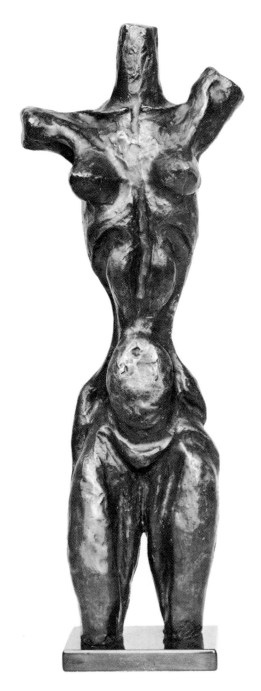

TORSO.
1967. Bronze. 20 high.

YOUNG MONK.
1952. Aluminum. 40 high.

BALLET.
1960. Bronze. 23 high.

MUSEUM COLLECTIONS

Addison Gallery of American Art, Andover, Massachusetts

Albion College, Albion, Michigan

Atlanta Art Association, Atlanta, Georgia

Brooks Memorial Art Gallery, Memphis, Tennessee

Busch-Reisinger Museum, Harvard University, Cambridge, Massachusetts

Cleveland Museum of Art, Cleveland, Ohio

Colby College, Waterville, Maine

Colorado Springs Fine Arts Center, Colorado Springs, Colorado

Dayton Art Institute, Dayton, Ohio

Des Moines Art Center, Des Moines, Iowa

Farnsworth Museum, Wellesley College, Wellesley, Massachusetts

Fort Worth Art Association, Fort Worth, Texas

Grand Rapids Art Museum, Grand Rapids, Michigan

Grinnell College, Grinnell, Iowa

Howard University, Washington, D.C.

Huntington Galleries, Huntington, West Virginia

Indiana University, Bloomington, Indiana

Kalamazoo Institute of Art, Kalamazoo, Michigan

La Casa Del Libro, San Juan, Puerto Rico

Lawrence Art Museum, Williams College, Williamstown, Massachusetts

Lyman Allyn Museum, New London, Connecticut

Madison Art Center, Madison, Wisconsin

Minneapolis Institute of Art, Minneapolis, Minnesota

Newark Museum of Art, Newark, New Jersey

Pennsylvania Academy of the Fine Arts, Philadelphia, Pennsylvania

Philadelphia Museum of Art, Philadelphia, Pennsylvania

Phoenix Museum of Art, Phoenix, Arizona

Portland Museum of Art, Portland, Maine

State University of New York, College at New Paltz, New York

Syracuse University Museum of Art, Syracuse, New York

Toronto Museum of Art, Toronto, Canada

University of Delaware, Newark, Delaware

University of Iowa, Iowa City, Iowa

University of Minnesota, Minneapolis, Minnesota

Utica Public Library, Utica, New York

Wadsworth Atheneum, Hartford, Connecticut

Whitney Museum of American Art, New York, New York

Wustum Museum of Fine Arts, Racine, Wisconsin

MOTHER AND CHILD.
1952. Bronze. 32 high.

RECLINING WOMAN, foot up.
1964. Bronze. 19 high.

RECLINING WOMAN.
1960. Bronze. 37 long.

SPIRIT OF HELEN KELLER.
1960. Bronze. 12 high.

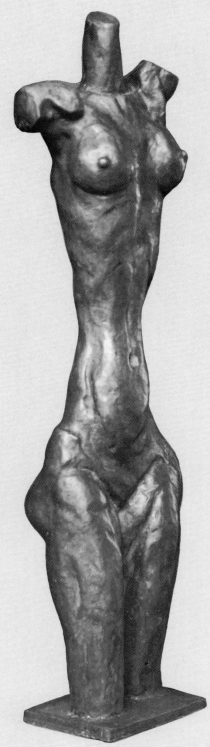

TORSO.
1953. Bronze. 65 high. Collections of the Whitney Museum
of American Art, New York, New York and Indiana University,
Bloomington, Indiana.

CATTLEYA.
1958. Bronze. 26 high.

DANCERS.
1963. Bronze. 21 high.

SEATED WOMAN, looking up.
1958. Bronze. 40 high. Collections of the Phoenix Museum of Art,
Phoenix, Arizona and the Wadsworth Atheneum,
Hartford, Connecticut.

CYPRIPEDIUM.
1959. Bronze. 22 high.

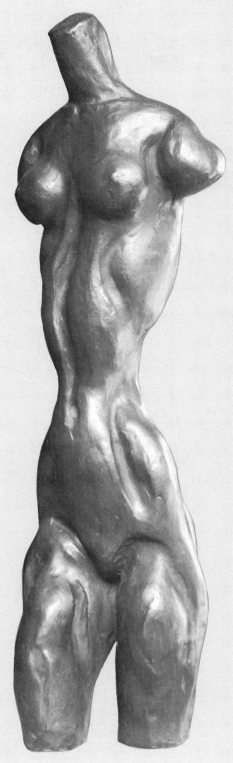

TORSO.
1957. Bronze. 15 high. Collection of the Portland
Museum of Art, Portland, Maine.

BALLET, no. 4.
1961. Bronze. 9 high.

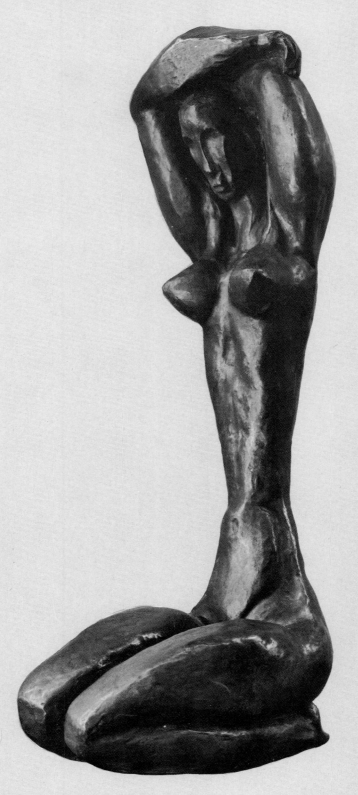

KNEELING WOMAN, arms raised.
1956. Bronze. 33 high.

CRUCIFIXION.
1960. Bronze. 32 high. Collection of St. John's Abbey,
Collegeville, Minnesota.

PRIVATE COLLECTIONS

Mr. and Mrs. Manville H. Abramson, Great Neck, New York

Mr. and Mrs. James S. Adams, Greenwich, Connecticut

Mr. Peter W. Adams, New York, New York

Dr. and Mrs. Jerome Adesman, Brooklyn, New York

American Foundation for the Overseas Blind, New York, New York

American Friends of the Hebrew University, New York, New York

Mr. and Mrs. Adam Aronson, St. Louis Missouri

Mr. and Mrs. Lester Francis Avnet, Kings Point, New York

Mr. and Mrs. S. Charles Baer, St. Louis, Missouri

Mr. and Mrs. Louis C. Baker, Greenwich, Connecticut

Mr. and Mrs. Lionel R. Bauman, Stamford, Connecticut

Mr. Mortimer Bauman, New York, New York

Mr. and Mrs. John I.H. Baur, Katonah, New York

Mr. and Mrs. Sidney B. Becker, New York, New York

Mrs. Mary Begley, New York, New York

Mr. and Mrs. Edwin A. Bergman, Chicago, Illinois

Mr. and Mrs. Herbert C. Bernard, New York, New York

Mr. and Mrs. William Adair Bernoudy, St. Louis, Missouri

Mr. and Mrs. Harold P. Bernstein, Great Neck, New York

Mr. Hobart D. Betts, Riverdale, New York

Mrs. Melvin A. Block, New York, New York

Mr. Lawrence H. Bloedel, Williamstown, Massachusetts

Mr. and Mrs. J. Boslow, Lawrence, New York

Mr. and Mrs. William Braden, Nevilly-Sur-Seine, France

Mr. Irvin Brenner, Pelham Manor, New York

Mrs. Lester Harris Brill, Highland Park, Illinois

Mrs. Samuel J. Briskin, Los Angeles, California

Mr. and Mrs. Alfred Bromberg, Dallas, Texas

Dr. and Mrs. Martin H. Bush, DeWitt, New York

Mr. and Mrs. James T. Canizaro, Jackson, Mississippi

Mr. and Mrs. Hugh Clark, Glenview, Illinois

Mr. John B. Clayburgh, Beverly Hills, California

Dr. and Mrs. Sidney Clyman, Scarsdale, New York

Mr. and Mrs. Sidney S. Cohen, St. Louis, Missouri

Dr. and Mrs. Arthur B. Coltman, Meadowbrook, Pennsylvania

Mr. and Mrs. John H. Cook, Litchfield, Connecticut

Mr. and Mrs. Gardner Cowles, New York, New York

Mr. and Mrs. Richard B. Cronheim, St. Louis, Missouri

Mr. and Mrs. Jerome Crossman, Dallas, Texas

Miss Nina Cullinan, Houston, Texas

Mr. and Mrs. Charles C. Cunningham, Kenilworth, Illinois

Miss Gertrude O. Danforth, Westwood, Massachusetts

Mr. and Mrs. Seth Dennis, Westport, Connecticut

Mr. and Mrs. Nathan Edward Derecktor, Katonah, New York

Mr. and Mrs. D. D'Eustachio, Pittsburgh, Pennsylvania

Mrs. Isabel W. Durcan, Katonah, New York

Mr. and Mrs. Grover D. Elliot, Purdy Station, New York

Mr. and Mrs. Francis M. Ellis, New York, New York

Mrs. John M. Ellis, Litchfield, Connecticut

Mr. Rudolph Ellis, Chappaqua, New York

Mr. Armand G. Erpf, New York, New York

Mr. Michael Erlanger, Redding, Connecticut

CROUCHING WOMAN.
1961. Brass. 3 high.

CATTLEYA, no. 2.
1960. Bronze. 27 high.

Mrs. Milton Erlanger, Oakhurst, New Jersey

Mr. and Mrs. Sandford G. Etherington, West Hartford, Connecticut

Carolyn Grant Fay, Houston, Texas

Dr. and Mrs. Benjamin Feingold, San Francisco, California

Laura and David Finn, New Rochelle, New York

Mr. and Mrs. Herbert Frank, St. Louis, Missouri

Mr. and Mrs. S. E. Freund, St. Louis, Missouri

Mrs. Rupert Fuller, Bedford Hills, New York

Mr. and Mrs. Andrew Gagarin, Litchfield, Connecticut

Mr. Woodie Garber, Cincinnati, Ohio

Mr. and Mrs. Milford Gerton, New York, New York

Mr. and Mrs. George Gibson, New York, New York

Mr. and Mrs. Richard L. Gilbert, New York, New York

Mr. and Mrs. Adam Gimbel, New York, New York

Mr. and Mrs. George Goldberg, Kings Point, New York

Mr. and Mrs. N. Lawrence Golden, Great Neck, New York

Dr. M. Goldschmidt, Zurich, Switzerland

Mr. Herbert L. Goldstein, New York, New York

Miss Marilyn Goodman, Great Neck, New York

Mr. Albert I. Gordon, New York, New York

Dr. and Mrs. Marshall B. Greenman, St. Louis, Missouri

Mr. and Mrs. Herman Gross, Great Neck, New York

Mr. Charles G. Hagedorn, Mamaroneck, New York

Mr. and Mrs. Sidney Harman, Old Westbury, New York

Mr. and Mrs. M. B. Harran, New York, New York

W. B. Harris and Miss Jane Grant, Litchfield, Connecticut

Dr. and Mrs. Edward F. Hartung, New York, New York

Mr. and Mrs. Robert J. Hausman, Scarsdale, New York

Mr. and Mrs. Julius Hertling, New York, New York

Mr. Fred S. Hill, Atlanta, Georgia

Mr. and Mrs. Maurice Hirsch, Sarasota, Florida

Mr. Bertram Hollander, New York, New York

Dr. and Mrs. E. J. Hornick, New York, New York

Dr. and Mrs. Aren Horowitz, Syosset, New York

Mrs. Arthur C. Hoskins, St. Louis, Missouri

Mr. and Mrs. Sigmund Hyman, Stevenson, Maryland

HEAD OF WOMAN.
1956. Bronze. 11 high.

ST. ANTHONY OF PADUA.
1963. Bronze. 24 high.

Sam and Mildred Jaffe, London, England

The Johnson Foundation, Racine, Wisconsin

Mrs. Earl M. Johnston, St. Louis, Missouri

Mrs. C. Maury Jones, Bedminster, New Jersey

Dr. and Mrs. Harold J. Joseph, St. Louis, Missouri

Mr. Frank Kacmarcik, St. Paul, Minnesota

Mr. and Mrs. Harold Kaplan, Verona, New Jersey

Mr. and Mrs. Arthur C. Kaufmann, Haverford, Pennsylvania

Miss Marion S. Kellogg, New York, New York

Miss Sybil Kennedy, New York, New York

Mr. Alfred W. Kleinbaum, New York, New York

Mr. and Mrs. Harry S. Koffman, Binghamton, New York

Mr. and Mrs. Edward F. Kook, New York, New York

Mr. and Mrs. Irwin Hamilton Kramer, New York, New York

Mr. and Mrs. Herbert S. Landau, Suffern, New York

Mr. Fred Lazarus III, Cincinnati, Ohio

Mr. Karl B. Leabo, New York, New York

Mr. and Mrs. Harry Lenart, Los Angeles, California

Mr. John Frank Lesser, Clayton, Missouri

Mrs. Marjorie Frank Lesser, Clayton, Missouri

Mr. and Mrs. Martin Levine, New York, New York

Mr. and Mrs. Max Levine, Houston, Texas

Mr. and Mrs. John David Levy, St. Louis, Missouri

Mr. and Mrs. Sidney Lichter, Scarsdale, New York

Mr. and Mrs. Charles E. Linsley, Litchfield, Connecticut

Mrs. Benjamin Loeb, St. Louis, Missouri

Mr. and Mrs. George Loeb, Rye, New York

Mr. and Mrs. Harry W. Loeb, St. Louis, Missouri

Mrs. V. Lynch-Staunton, Nashville, Ontario, Canada

Mr. and Mrs. David Mallimson, Great Neck, New York

Mr. and Mrs. Charles J. Malmed, Great Neck, New York

Mr. Joseph Mandelbaum, Brooklyn, New York

Mr. and Mrs. Fredric March, New York, New York

Dr. and Mrs. David N. Marks, New York, New York

Dr. and Mrs. Martin G. Marmon, Scarsdale, New York

Mr. David May, Beverly Hills, California

ST. BERNARD OF CLAIRVAUX TEACHING.
1959. Bronze. 54 high. Collection of St. Bernard's Church,
Hazardville, Connecticut.

141

HORIZON.
1966. Bronze. 15 high.

Mrs. Tom May, Beverly Hills, California

Mrs. William B. Mayne, Roslyn Heights, New York

Dr. and Mrs. Frederick Mebel, Rockville Center, New York

Mr. and Mrs. H. L. Meckler, Kings Point, New York

Mr. and Mrs. S. J. Mehlman, London, England

Mr. and Mrs. Abraham Melnick, Great Neck, New York

Mr. and Mrs. Lawrence A. Meyers, New York, New York

Mr. and Mrs. Morris Moscowitz, St. Louis, Missouri

Mr. and Mrs. Harry L. Nair, West Hartford, Connecticut

Mrs. Richard Nardella, Glendale, New York

Mr. and Mrs. Clarence Obletz, Buffalo, New York

Mr. Henry Ohring, West Orange, New Jersey

Mr. and Mrs. William A. Perry, Framingham, Massachusetts

Mr. and Mrs. Henry B. Pflager, St. Louis, Missouri

Mr. and Mrs. Ned L. Pines, New York, New York

Mary Gardner Preminger, Malibu, California

Mr. W. A. Reilly, Dover, Massachusetts

Mr. Charles Renthal, New York, New York

Mr. Harry A. Richards, Stamford, Connecticut

Dr. and Mrs. Benjamin Rosenberg, Brooklyn, New York

Mr. and Mrs. Charles S. Rosenthal, New York, New York

Mr. and Mrs. Norman Rubinstein, Queens Village, New York

Saint Paul's School, Concord, Massachusetts

Mr. and Mrs. Alexander E. Salzman, New York, New York

Mr. and Mrs. Theodore Samuels, St. Louis, Missouri

Mr. and Mrs. Albert H. Sanders, Great Neck, New York

Mr. and Mrs. David Saul, Atlanta, Georgia

Mr. and Mrs. Richard Scheuch, West Hartford, Connecticut

Mr. Gabriel Semo, New York, New York

Mr. and Mrs. Warren Shapleigh, St. Louis, Missouri

Mr. and Mrs. Sidney M. Shoenberg, Jr., St. Louis, Missouri

Mr. and Mrs. Morris Shor, Elizabeth, New Jersey

Mr. and Mrs. Frank Silverman, Chicago, Illinois

Mr. and Mrs. Edgar Sinton, Hillsborough, California

Mr. and Mrs. Richard Solomon, New York, New York

Mr. and Mrs. Saul Solomon, New York, New York

STANDING WOMAN.
1968. Bronze. 55 high.

Mr. and Mrs. Sidney L. Solomon, New York, New York

Mr. and Mrs. Benjamin Sonnenberg, New York, New York

Dr. and Mrs. Burton B. Steel, New York, New York

Mr. and Mrs. James B. Stuart, New York, New York

Mr. and Mrs. Louis Tiger, St. Louis, Missouri

Trade Bank and Trust Company, New York, New York

Mr. and Mrs. Richard W. Trattler, Brookville, New York

Mr. and Mrs. Peter Trier, Waterbury, Connecticut

Mr. and Mrs. Percy Uris, New York, New York

Walden School, New York, New York

Mr. and Mrs. David Wall, London, England

Dr. and Mrs. Alfred E. Wallis, Forest Hills, New York

Mr. and Mrs. George Walter, Shorewood, Wisconsin

Mr. and Mrs. Lew Wasserman, Beverly Hills, California

Dr. and Mrs. Milton Weg, West Orange, New Jersey

Mr. and Mrs. H. Weltchek, Elizabeth, New Jersey

Mr. Arthur Weyhe, New York, New York

Mr. Erhard Weyhe, New York, New York

Leonie Migeon White, Roxbury, Connecticut

Mr. and Mrs. Joseph S. Wohl, Lawrence, New York

Mr. and Mrs. A. B. Wolosoff, Great Neck, New York

Young Women's Hebrew Association, Elizabeth, New Jersey

Mr. and Mrs. Leonard Zahn, Kings Point, New York

Dr. and Mrs. Jerry Zaslow, Elkins Park, Pennsylvania

Mrs. Ruth Zierler, Freeport, New York

Although more than 500 private collectors own Doris Caesar's sculptures, only those individuals who could be located and granted permission to use their names are included in this list.

HEAD.
1959. Bronze. 14 high.

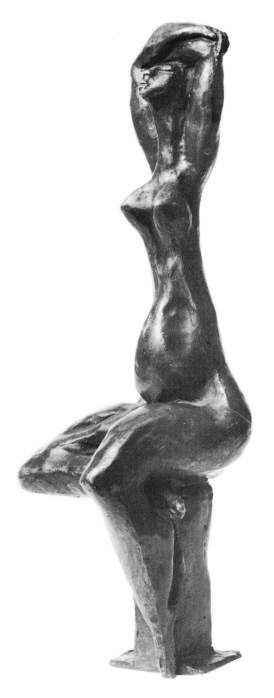

WOMAN, on a pedestal.
1959. Bronze. 15 high.

NOTES

1. Goodrich, Lloyd, and Baur, John I. H. *Four American Expressionists* (Frederick A. Praeger, New York: 1959), 23-24. Hereafter cited as *Four American Expressionists*.

2. *Four American Expressionists,* 27.

3. Doris Caesar's Notebooks, Doris Caesar Collection, Syracuse University.

4. Alexander Archipenko to Doris Caesar, December 4, 1931, Doris Caesar Collection, Syracuse University.

5. Caesar, Doris. *Phantom Thoughts* (G. P. Putnam's Sons, New York: 1934), 49.

6. Doris Caesar's Notebooks, Doris Caesar Collection, Syracuse University.

7. *Ibid.*

8. *Four American Expressionists,* 30.

9. Doris Caesar's Notebooks, Doris Caesar Collection, Syracuse University.

10. *Four American Expressionists*, 34.

11. *Ibid.*

12. *Ibid.*

13. Doris Caesar's Notebooks, Doris Caesar Collection, Syracuse University.

14. John I. H. Baur to Doris Caesar, March 9, 1961, Doris Caesar Collection, Syracuse University.

15. Doris Caesar to the Right Reverend Baldwin Dworschak, February, 1963, Doris Caesar Collection, Syracuse University.

16. Doris Caesar to Father Prior Benedict Reid, November, 1964, Doris Caesar Collection, Syracuse University.

17. *Ibid.*

18. *Ibid.*

19. Father Prior Benedict Reid to Doris Caesar, January, 1965, Doris Caesar Collection, Syracuse University.

THE PATRIARCH.
1967. Bronze. 36 high.

KNEELING WOMAN.
1968. Bronze. 35 high.

SELECTED BIBLIOGRAPHY

MANUSCRIPTS

Doris Caesar Papers, Syracuse University.

BOOKS AND
EXHIBITION CATALOGUES

Baur, John I.H. *Doris Caesar.* Washington: Howard University, 1958. (Catalogue of exhibition of sculpture, March 2—April 8, 1958.)

Baur, John I.H. *Woman In Sculpture By Doris Caesar.* Boston: Margaret Brown Gallery, 1956. (Catalogue of exhibition of sculpture, October 29—November 24, 1956.)

Caesar. New York: Weyhe Gallery, 1964. (Catalogue of exhibition of sculpture, February—March, 1964.)

Caesar. New York: Weyhe Gallery, 1969. (Catalogue of exhibition of sculpture, February—March, 1969.)

Caesar, Doris. *Certain Paths.* New York: G.P. Putnam's Sons, 1934.

Caesar, Doris. *Phantom Thoughts.* New York: G.P. Putnam's Sons, 1934.

Chamson, Andre. *New York Six.* Paris: Petit Palais, 1950. (Catalogue of exhibition of sculpture, June—August, 1950.)

Cunningham, Charles C. *Doris Caesar, Philip Evergood.* Hartford: Wadsworth Atheneum, 1960. (Catalogue of sculpture and paintings, August 3—September 11, 1960.)

Doris Caesar. New York: Weyhe Gallery, 1947. (Catalogue of exhibition of sculpture, March 4—March 26, 1947.)

Doris Caesar. New York: Weyhe Gallery, 1959. (Catalogue of exhibition of sculpture, January 15—February 7, 1959.)

Doris Caesar. Philadelphia: Crillon Galleries, 1932. (Catalogue of exhibition of sculpture, November 28—December 12, 1932.)

Doris Porter Caesar. New York: Montross Gallery, 1931. (Catalogue of exhibition of sculpture, November 30—December 12, 1931.)

Goodrich, Lloyd and Baur, John I.H. *Between the Fairs, 25 Years of American Art*, 1939 to 1964. New York: Whitney Museum of American Art, 1964. (Catalogue of an exhibition held at the Whitney, June 24—September 23, 1964.)

Goodrich, Lloyd and Baur, John I.H. *Four American Expressionists*: *Doris Caesar, Chaim Gross, Karl Knaths, Abraham Rattner.* New York: Frederick A. Praeger, 1959.

Goodrich, Lloyd and Baur, John I.H. *Four American Expressionists*: *Doris Caesar, Chaim Gross, Karl Knaths, Abraham Rattner*. New York: Whitney Museum of American Art, 1959. (Catalogue of Whitney Museum of American Art Annual Exhibition, January 14—March 1, 1959.)

Hayes, Bartlett H. *Caesar*. New York: Weyhe Gallery, 1957. (Catalogue of loan exhibition of small sculpture, 1927—1957, October 14—November 23, 1957.)

More, Hermon. *1951 Annual Exhibition*. New York: Whitney Museum of American Art, 1951. (Catalogue of annual exhibition of sculpture, watercolors and drawings, March 17—May 6, 1951.)

Sculpture By Doris Caesar. New York: Buchholz Gallery, 1943. (Catalogue of exhibition of sculpture, September 28—October 16, 1943.)

Sculpture By Doris Caesar. New York: Weyhe Gallery, 1935. (Catalogue of exhibition of sculpture, April 8—April 27, 1935.)

Sculpture By Doris Caesar. New York: Weyhe Gallery, 1937. (Catalogue of exhibition of sculpture, March 1—20,1937.)

Sculpture By Doris Caesar. New York: Weyhe Gallery, 1939. (Catalogue of exhibition of sculpture, March 6—25, 1939.)

Weyhe, Erhard. *Caesar*. New York: Weyhe Gallery, 1952. (Catalogue of exhibition of sculpture, December 15, 1952—January 20, 1953.)

NEWSPAPERS AND PERIODICALS

"A Sculpture Show." *New York Herald Tribune*. (March 7, 1937.)

Adlow, Dorothy. "Artists of Vigor, Poetry, and Delight." *The Christian Science Monitor*. (January 31, 1959.)

"Americans." *The New York Times*. (March 7, 1937.)

"Art in New York." *Time*. (April 7, 1967.)

Art News. (March 11, 1939.)

Ashley, Roberta. "New York Art Goes To Paris." *New York Herald Tribune*. (July 9, 1950.)

Askew, Rual. "Exhibitions Hit Extremes." *The Dallas Morning News*. (December, 1959.)

Berkham, Florence. "Also Sculpture Show at the Wadsworth." *The Hartford Times*. (August 13, 1960.)

Blair, Date. "Museum Offers Two Exhibits For Christmas Holidays." *The Dallas Times Herald.* (December 20, 1959.)

Breuning, Margaret. *Art Digest*. (May 1, 1951.)

Buckley, Charles E. "Expressionists in Art Subject Talk." *Union Leader.* Manchester, New Hampshire. (May 1, 1959.)

Burrows, Carlyle. "Audubon." *New York Herald Tribune*. (January 22, 1961.)

Burrows, Carlyle. *New York Herald Tribune*. (March 9, 1947.)

Burrows, Carlyle. *New York Herald Tribune*. (October 23, 1960.)

Burrows, Carlyle. *New York Herald Tribune*. (March 12, 1961.)

Burrows, Carlyle. "Sculpture Show In Many Styles." *New York Herald Tribune*. (October 22, 1961.)

"Caesar." *The New York Times*. (February 2, 1964.)

"Caesar." *The New York Times*. (June 7, 1964.)

"Caesar at the Weyhe Gallery." *Art Voices*. (March, 1964.)

Coates, Robert M. "The Art Galleries: Mixed Company." *The New Yorker*. (December 13, 1958.)

"Crillon Galleries," *Philadelphia Record*. (December 4, 1932.)

"Crillon Galleries In New Quarters." *Philadelphia Public Ledger*. (December 4, 1932.)

Cureau, Doris. "Sculptor's Art Graces Hazardville Church." *The Hartford Times*. (November 7, 1959.)

Devree, Howard. "American Variety." *The New York Times*. (May 5, 1957.)

Devree, Howard. "Chiefly Modern." *The New York Times*. (April 9, 1950.)

Devree, Howard. "Diverse Americans." *The New York Times*. (January 18, 1959.)

Devree, Howard. "Doris Caesar Displays Sculpture." *The New York Times*. (October 17, 1957.)

Devree, Howard. "Four Expressionists." *The New York Times*. (January 26, 1959.)

Devree, Howard. *Magazine of Art*. (April, 1937.)

Devree, Howard. "Modern Representation to Abstraction by Pre-Columbians in New Shows." *The New York Times*. (May 5, 1957.)

Devree, Howard. "Pennsylvania Academy Opens Its Annual." *The New York Times*. (January 14, 1959.)

Devree, Howard. "Sculpture Round-Up." *The New York Times*. (December 9, 1951.)

Devree, Howard. "Thirty-Second Annual Exhibition." *The New York Times.* (December 12, 1956.)

Devree, Howard. "Whitney Annual Raises the Question of the Basis of Selection." *The New York Times*. (November 24, 1957.)

"Doris Caesar." *Art News*. (March, 1947.)

"Doris Caesar." *Art News*. (January, 1959.)

"Doris Caesar." *Art News*. (February, 1964.)

"Doris Caesar." *Art News*. (May, 1946.)

"Doris Caesar." *New York Herald Tribune*. (February 2, 1964.)

"Doris Caesar, Once a Pupil of Archipenko." *The New York Times*. (April 10, 1935.)

"Doris Caesar Sculptures." *Art Digest*. (October 1, 1943.)

"Doris Caesar's Sculptures." *The New York Sun*. (March 4, 1937.)

"Doris Caesar's Sculpture." *New York World-Telegram*. (March 6, 1937.)

"Doris Caesar's Sixth." *Art Digest*. (February 15, 1940.)

"Doris Caesar's Strong and Emotional Sculptures." *Art News*. (March 2, 1940.)

"Doris Caesar Turns to Poetry." *The Poetry Review*. (August, 1937.)

"Expressionist Art." *The Westchester Post*. (December 21, 1950.)

"Expressionists in Art Subject of Gallery Talk." *Union Leader*. Manchester, New Hampshire. (May 1, 1959.)

Fransioli, Thomas. "Doris Caesar's Work at Sharon Gallery." *The Lakeville Journal*. (August 10, 1961.)

Genauer, Emily. "Abstract Art Still Dominates Famous Survey." *New York Herald Tribune*. (November 24, 1957.)

Genauer, Emily. "Art: Whitney Annual of Sculpture." *New York Herald Tribune*. (December 11, 1960.)

Genauer, Emily. "Intensity in Sculpture." *New York World-Telegram*. (March 22, 1947.)

Genauer, Emily, "'Isms' Is Theme of Two New Art Shows." *New York Herald Tribune*. (January 18, 1959.)

Genauer, Emily. *New York Herald Tribune*. (January 21, 1951.)

Gibbs, Jo. "Doris Caesar Presents Eloquent Sculpture." *Art Digest*. (March 1, 1947.)

Hannon, Robert E. "Dedication Rite at New Priory Church." *St. Louis Post-Dispatch*. (September 23, 1962.)

"Helen Keller, at 80, Still Helps." *The New York Times*. (June 28. 1960.)

Hindman, Frank T. (Mrs.) "Religious Art Exhibit to Open." *Memphis Press-Scimitar*. (August 31, 1960.)

"Introduction to New Art at St. John's." *St. Paul Pioneer Press*. (January 5, 1964.)

Jewell, Edward Alden. "Doris Caesar." *The New York Times*. (April 23, 1933.)

Jewell, Edward Alden. "Modernism—Sculpture—Drawings." *The New York Times*. (March 9, 1947.)

Jewell, Edward Alden. *The New York Times*. (February 25, 1940.)

Jewell, Edward Alden. *The New York Times*. (October 3, 1943.)

Krauss, William A. "Books and Bookmen." *The Bergen Evening Record*. (November 10, 1937.)

Kruse, A.Z. "American Sculptress." *The Brooklyn Eagle*. (February 25, 1940.)

Kruse, A.Z. "Sculptures by Doris Caesar." *The Brooklyn Eagle*. (March 12, 1939.)

Lewis, Emory. "Four at the Whitney." *Cue*. (January 10, 1959.)

"Merit Found in Sculptures by Doris Caesar." *New York World-Telegram*. (April 13, 1935.)

"Modern Sculptors." *Art Digest*. (December 1, 1950.)

New York American. (April 22, 1933.)

New York Evening Post. (April 22, 1933.)

New York Herald Tribune. (April 23, 1933.)

Northrop, Guy. "Flowering of Religious Art Today Revealed in Madonna Circle Show." *The Commercial Appeal*. Memphis. Tennessee. (September 4, 1960.)

O'Doherty, Brian. "Doris Caesar." *The New York Times*. (February 22, 1964.)

Pascone, T. "Artist, Sculptor 'Splash' Color, Rhythm." *The Hartford Times*. (August 4, 1960.)

"Prayer of Guidance." *Liturgical Arts.* May, 1959.)

Preston, Stuart. "Quartet of Sculptors." *The New York Times*. (March 12, 1961.)

Preston, Stuart. "Sculpture Annual." *The New York Times*. (March 26, 1950.)

Reed, Judith Kaye. "Distaff Sculpture." *Art Digest*. (March 1, 1950.)

"Rough Surfaced Sculpture." *Art Digest.* (May 1, 1933.)

"St. John's World of Art." *St. Paul Sunday Pioneer Press*. (January 5, 1964.)

"Saint Teresa." *The Hartford Courant*. (October 17, 1966.)

Schiff, Bennett. "In the Art Galleries . . ." *New York Post*. (January, 1959.)

Schwartz, Marvin D. "Doris Caesar at the Weyhe Gallery" *Apollo*. (February, 1959.)

"Sculptures By Doris Caesar." *New York Herald Tribune*. (April 14, 1935.)

"Six Sculptors at Argent." *Art Digest*. (June 1, 1948.)

"Six Women Sculptors." *Art News*. (Summer, 1948.)

"Some Sculptures." *Art Digest*. (March 15, 1937.)

"Studies In Sculpture." *Country Life*. (October, 1931.)

The Brooklyn Eagle. (April 16, 1933.)

The New York Sun. (April 22, 1933.)

The Philadelphia Inquirer. (December 4, 1932.)

"The Whitney's Sculpture Court." *Newsweek*. (October 3, 1966.)

"Two Sculptures: Caesar Art Receives Accolades in Trieste." *The Litchfield Enquirer*. (October 20, 1966.)

"Two Young Sculptors Show Work of Much Promise." *New York Post*. (April 13, 1935.)

"Vogue's Spot-Light." *Vogue.* (April 15, 1933.)

"Wadsworth Atheneum, Hartford Exhibition." *The New York Times.* (August 14, 1960.)

"Wadsworth Gallery to Exhibit Works of 2 State Artists." *New Haven Sunday Register.* (July 31, 1960.)

PHOTOGRAPHIC CREDITS

INDEX